Inseparable

ROMANS 8

New Community Bible Study Series

Old Testament
   Exodus: Journey toward God
   The Ten Commandments: Laws That Liberate
   1–2 Samuel: Growing a Heart for God
   Nehemiah: Overcoming Challenges
   Psalms Vol. 1: Encountering God
   Psalms Vol. 2: Life-Changing Lessons
   Daniel: Pursuing Integrity
New Testament
   Sermon on the Mount 1: Connect with God
   Sermon on the Mount 2: Connect with Others
   The Lord's Prayer: Praying with Power
   Parables: Imagine Life God's Way
   The Passion Story: Uphill Faith
   Luke: Lessons from Jesus
   Acts: Build Community
   Romans: Find Freedom
   Romans 8: Inseparable
   2 Corinthians: Serving from the Heart
   Philippians: Run the Race
   Colossians: Discover the New You
   Titus: Spiritual Influence
   James: Live Wisely
   1 Peter: Stand Strong
   1 John: Love Each Other
   Revelation: Experience God's Power

BILL HYBELS
WITH KEVIN AND SHERRY HARNEY

New Community
KNOWING. LOVING. SERVING. CELEBRATING.

Inseparable
ROMANS 8

ZONDERVAN.com/
AUTHORTRACKER
follow your favorite authors

ZONDERVAN

Romans 8: Inseparable
Copyright © 2009 by Willow Creek Association

ISBN 978-0-310-28059-0

Cover and interior design by Sherri Hoffman

Printed in the United States of America

10 11 12 13 14 15 • 21 20 19 18 17 16 15 14 13 12 11 10 9 8 7 6 5 4 3 2

CONTENTS

New Community Bible Study Series   6

Introduction   11

Session 1
The No Condemnation Concept—Romans 8:1–11   15

Session 2
Confident Christians—Romans 8:12–17   26

Session 3
Only One Life—Romans 8:18–27   35

Session 4
Our Lifeline in Times of Trouble—Romans 8:28   45

Session 5
God Is for You—Romans 8:31–34   54

Session 6
More Than Conquerors—Romans 8:35–39   64

Leader's Notes   74

God has created us for community. This need is built into the very fiber of our being, the DNA of our spirit. As Christians, our deepest desire is to see the truth of God's Word as it influences our relationships with others. We long for a dynamic encounter with God's Word, intimate closeness with his people, and radical transformation of our lives. But how can we accomplish those three difficult tasks?

The New Community Bible Study Series creates a place for all of this to happen. In-depth Bible study, community-building opportunities, and life-changing applications are all built into every session of this small group study guide.

How to Build Community

How do we build a strong, healthy Christian community? The whole concept for this study grows out of a fundamental understanding of Christian community that is dynamic and transformational. We believe that Christians don't simply gather to exchange doctrinal affirmations. Rather, believers are called by God to get into each other's lives. We are family, for better or for worse, and we need to connect with each other.

Community is not built through sitting in the same building and singing the same songs. It is forged in the fires of life. When we know each other deeply—the good, the bad, and the ugly—community is experienced. Community grows when we learn to rejoice with one another, celebrating life. Roots grow deep when we know we are loved by others and are free to extend love to them as well. Finally, community deepens and is built when we commit to serve each other and let others serve us. This process of doing ministry and humbly receiving the ministry of others is critical for healthy community life.

Build Community Through Knowing and Being Known

We all long to know others deeply and to be fully known by them. Although we might run from this level of intimacy at times, we all want to have people in our lives who trust us enough to disclose the deep and tender parts of themselves. In turn, we want to reveal some of our feelings, expressing them freely to people we trust.

The first section of each of these six studies creates a place for deep knowing and being known. Through serious reflection on the truth of Scripture, you will be invited to communicate parts of your heart and life with your small group members. You might even discover yourself opening parts of your heart that you have thus far kept hidden. The Bible study and discussion questions do not encourage surface conversation. The only way to go deep in knowing others and being known by them is to dig deep, and this takes work. Knowing others also takes trust — that you will honor each other and respect each other's confidences.

Build Community Through Celebrating and Being Celebrated

If you have not had a good blush recently, read a short book in the Bible called Song of Songs. It's a record of a bride and groom writing poetic and romantic love letters to each other. They are freely celebrating every conceivable aspect of each other's personality, character, and physical appearance. At one point the groom says, "You have made my heart beat fast with a single glance from your eyes." Song of Songs is a reckless celebration of life, love, and all that is good.

We need to recapture the joy and freedom of celebration. In every session of this study, your group will commit to celebrate together. Although there are many ways to express joy, we will let our expression of celebration come through prayer. In each session you will take time to come before the God of joy and celebrate who he is and what he is doing. You will also have opportunity to celebrate what God is doing in your life and the lives of those who are a part of your small group. You will become a community of affirmation, celebration, and joy through your prayer time together.

You will need to be sensitive during this time of prayer together. Not everyone feels comfortable praying with a group of people. Be aware that each person is starting at a different place in their freedom to pray in a group, so be patient. Seek to promote a warm and welcoming atmosphere where each person can stretch a little and learn what it means to be a community that celebrates with God in the center.

Build Community Through Loving and Being Loved

Unless we are exchanging deeply committed levels of love with a few people, we will die slowly on the inside. This is precisely why so many people feel almost nothing at all. If we don't learn to exchange love with family and friends, we will eventually grow numb and no longer believe love is even a possibility. This is not God's plan. He hungers for us to be loved and to give love to others. As a matter of fact, he wants this for us even more than we want it for ourselves.

Every session in this study will address the area of loving and being loved. You will be challenged, in your personal life and as a small group, to be intentional and consistent about building loving relationships. You will get practical tools and be encouraged to set measurable goals for giving and receiving love.

Build Community Through Serving and Being Served

Community is about serving and humbly allowing others to serve you. The single most stirring example of this is recorded in John 13, where Jesus takes the position of the lowest servant and washes the feet of his followers. He gives them a powerful example and then calls them to follow. Servanthood is at the very core of community. To sustain deep relationships over a long period of time, there must be humility and a willingness to serve each other.

At the close of each session will be a clear challenge to servanthood. As a group, and as individual followers of Christ, you will discover that community is built through serving others. You will also find that your own small group members will grow in their ability to extend service to your life.

Bible Study Basics

To get the most out of this study, you will need to prepare and participate. Here are some guidelines to help you.

Preparing for the Study

1. If possible, even if you are not the leader, look over each session before you meet, read the Bible passages, and answer the questions. The more you are prepared, the more you will gain from the study.
2. Begin your preparation with prayer. Ask God to help you understand the passage and apply it to your life.
3. A good modern translation, such as the New International Version, Today's New International Version, the New American Standard Bible, or the New Revised Standard Version, will give you the most help. Questions in this guide are based on the New International Version.
4. Read and reread the passages. You must know what the passage says before you can understand what it means and how it applies to you.
5. Write your answers in the spaces provided in the study guide. This will help you participate more fully in the discussion and will also help you personalize what you are learning.
6. Keep a Bible dictionary handy to look up unfamiliar words, names, or places.

Participating in the Study

1. Be willing to join in the discussion. The leader of the group will not be lecturing but will encourage people to discuss what they have learned in the passage. Plan to share what God has taught you during your preparation time.
2. Stick to the passages being studied. Base your answers on the verses being discussed rather than on outside authorities such as commentaries or your favorite author or speaker.

3. Try to be sensitive to the other members of the group. Listen attentively when they speak, and be affirming whenever you can. This will encourage more hesitant members of the group to participate.
4. Be careful not to dominate the discussion. By all means participate, but allow others to have equal time.
5. If you are a discussion leader or a participant who wants further insights, you will find additional comments in the Leader's Notes at the back of the book.

Romans 8:
Inseparable

Favorite and Famous Passages

In 2 Timothy 3:16 the apostle Paul writes, "All Scripture is God-breathed and is useful for teaching, rebuking, correcting and training in righteousness." This means that every book of the Bible, every chapter, every verse is given by the Spirit of God and has power to impact our lives. From the first verse of Genesis to the final verse of Revelation, it is all the Word of God! Yet certain passages seem to capture the hearts and imaginations of God's people and become famous and favorite texts. Consider these much loved and recognized verses:

> I consider that our present sufferings are not worth comparing with the glory that will be revealed in us.

> And we know that in all things God works for the good of those who love him, who have been called according to his purpose.

> For I am convinced that neither death nor life, neither angels nor demons, neither the present nor the future, nor any powers, neither height nor depth, nor anything else in all creation, will be able to separate us from the love of God that is in Christ Jesus our Lord.

> For you did not receive a spirit that makes you a slave again to fear, but you received the Spirit of sonship. And by him we cry, "Abba, Father."

> The Spirit himself testifies with our spirit that we are God's children.

> In the same way, the Spirit helps us in our weakness. We do not know what we ought to pray for, but the Spirit

himself intercedes for us with groans that words cannot express.

What, then, shall we say in response to this? If God is for us, who can be against us?

Therefore, there is now no condemnation for those who are in Christ Jesus.

Would it surprise you to discover that all of these passages are found in one book of the Bible? What if you were to find out that all eight are from just one chapter in the Bible? Well, they are. Every one of these powerful and memorable texts comes from Romans 8.

Many scholars and Christians consider the eighth chapter of Romans to be the single most important chapter in all of the apostle Paul's writings. That is quite a distinction when you realize that Paul's writings compose approximately two-thirds of the New Testament. So many classic verses appear in this one single chapter in God's Word.

Inseparable

Romans 8 contains many wonderful themes, but one of the clearest and most gripping is the message that nothing can separate us from the love of God. If we have entered an authentic relationship with God the Father through faith in Jesus Christ, we are bonded to him with ties that no one and nothing can break. Paul puts it this way:

For I am convinced that neither death nor life, neither angels nor demons, neither the present nor the future, nor any powers, neither height nor depth, nor anything else in all creation, will be able to separate us from the love of God that is in Christ Jesus our Lord. (Romans 8:38–39)

In a world where everything seems to be coming unraveled, these words bring hope, strength, and comfort to the heart of a Christ follower. Everywhere we look, brokenness seems to be growing. Couples stand at the altar and say, "Until death do us part," but a few years later the marriage ends. Musical groups make an album or two, enter the public spotlight, and then break up. Professional sports figures seem to have little devotion to one team anymore; when they can make a few more bucks with another franchise, they are packed up and out of town. Friendships hit tough times and people just walk away.

Into a world where separation, betrayal, and brokenness are the norm, God speaks. In Christ, we can be connected to the heart of the Father with inseparable love. Nothing can make God stop loving us. No one can snatch us from the Father's hand (John 10:29). In Christ, we are loved, secure, safe.

When we read Romans 8 through this lens, life begins to make sense again, hope rises like the sun after a dark cold night, and we can almost feel the strong arms of the Father wrap around us. We remember that we are loved children and our Father will never let go of us.

These six sessions will create a place for you to learn the truth that nothing can separate you from God's love. But, more than understanding this message, you will have moments when you encounter this God. You will look into his fatherly face and realize the depth of his love and the strength of the heavenly arms that are wrapped securely around you . . . today and forever.

The No Condemnation Concept

ROMANS 8:1–11

If you don't know the sport of hockey, or if you are a casual viewer, you might get the impression that there aren't many rules, and that the players can indiscriminately hit each other with their sticks and fists. That is simply not the case. Hockey does allow a fair amount of physical contact — it's part of the game. But there are many rules that are quite specific, and if a player breaks one of them he is sent to what's called the penalty box.

Depending on the infraction, a player is banned from the ice for a certain amount of time and forced to sit in the penalty box. Once he has "served his time," he may return to the ice, and get back into the game.

Even if you have never played hockey, there is a chance you have spent time in a spiritual penalty box. You have broken one of God's rules (sinned in some way) and decided that you needed to spend some time off the ice, out of the game. You figure you're disqualified from walking with Jesus, serving him, experiencing joy, having peace, or living in his power — at least until you have done "penance" and deserve to be back in God's good graces. During these precious hours, days, months, and even years Christians can squander their lives sitting on the spiritual sidelines of life.

For many followers of Jesus, this process of calling a foul on themselves and spending time in the penalty box can actually *feel* spiritual. But how can we know the right amount of time to mope around, feel bad, beat ourselves up, and stay in the penalty box? What is the appropriate time-out penalty for each infraction against God's holiness? When is the condemnation over? When are we allowed back in the game?

If we are going to play the penalty box game, it might be helpful to have some guidelines. First, we need to identify how to feel and act during our time in the penalty box. Try these:

- We feel guilty and condemned,
- We lose our joy,
- We feel far from God,
- We distance ourselves (physically and emotionally) from other believers and don't fellowship with them,
- We disqualify ourselves from service and ministry,
- We do things to prove to God that we deserve his grace and an invitation back into the game.

Second, we need to clarify how long we should consign ourselves to the penalty box for specific infractions. Consider these possibilities:

- When you get mad at a family member or friend — forty-five minutes in the penalty box,
- Each time you tell a little lie (for instance, the phone rings and you say, "Tell her I'm not here") — thirty minutes in the penalty box,
- When you tell a big lie (maybe you fudge the numbers on your income tax) — five days in the penalty box,
- You lust in your heart — four hours in the penalty box,
- You act on your lust and commit some act of sexual immorality — four months in the penalty box.

Is this all beginning to sound a bit silly? I hope so!

Because of the grace of Jesus we don't have to walk around feeling condemned, discouraged, and guilty. We no longer need to waste hours, days, and weeks disqualifying ourselves from service, fellowship, and God's joy. Jesus came to set us free from these kinds of spiritual games. In Christ's grace, we don't have to spend one more second in the penalty box.

Making the Connection

1. As you look back on your Christian journey thus far, describe one penalty box experience. (What does your penalty box look like and how long do you tend to put yourself there?)

Knowing and Being Known

Read Romans 8:1 – 11

2. What does the apostle Paul have to say to those who are prone to put themselves in a spiritual penalty box every time they commit a sin?

What has God done to deal with the reality of our sin and the consequences of it?

3. Paul draws vivid and clear distinctions between what it looks like when we live according to our sinful nature as opposed to living according to the Spirit of God. What does it look like when we live according to the sinful nature?

What does it look like when we live according to the Spirit of God?

How do these two lifestyles battle against each other?

The Payment of Jesus ... Getting Out of the Penalty Box

When we sin, most of us say in our heart, "Oh, no! I'm sure God is ticked off and wants me to be in the penalty box now." We recognize our disobedience and strongly sense that we deserve some kind of punishment. This is a very common response.

Jesus sadly shakes his head when he observes such self-condemnation. The Word of God declares it so clearly: "There is now no condemnation for those who are in Christ Jesus." The holy One of heaven, Jesus Christ, says, "I don't condemn you!" So, here is the million-dollar question: *Who are we to condemn ourselves?*

In these moments we must listen to the rock-solid teaching of Scripture and the voice of Jesus. Each time we are about to head to the penalty box, Jesus wants to remind us of what he did so we could live without condemnation: he died on the cross ... he rose again ... he paid the price ... he said, "It is finished!" He does not desire our passive inaction of sitting on the sidelines for days or weeks. Instead, he calls us to Spirit-led action. Confess your sin. Repent and turn away from it. Make things right with those you have hurt. Stay connected with God, remain in fellowship, and keep pressing forward. Take the nail-scarred hand of your Savior and walk on! Don't waste one more moment of your life in the penalty box.

Read Romans 8:1 – 4; Mark 10:24 – 34; and Hebrews 10:11 – 14

4. In light of the teaching in these three passages, what do you think Jesus would say to those who are in the habit of putting themselves into a spiritual penalty box every time they sin?

When Jesus sees you sitting in your own self-appointed penalty box, how do you think he feels?

5. Those who are in the habit of condemning themselves every time they sin and struggle to follow God's plan for their life can feel like they are doing a good thing. The problem is, sitting around and feeling condemned is not the same as repenting and walking in greater obedience. Shift your mind into theologian mode and respond to *one* of the following questions, each of which addresses a theological implication of putting ourselves in a spiritual penalty box:

   • How can putting yourself in a spiritual penalty box actually get in the way of true repentance?

   • If you condemn yourself for sin when God's Word says, "There is now no condemnation," what are you saying about your view of the Bible?

   • When Jesus was dying on the cross he declared, "It is finished." What are we saying about the price Jesus paid on the cross when we heap additional punishment on ourselves?

6. How might your life change if, from this moment on, you never spent another minute in the spiritual penalty box?

What needs to shift in your thinking for this to become a reality?

The Heart of the Father ... Restored Relationship

Jesus said, "For God did not send his Son into the world to condemn the world, but to save the world through him" (John 3:17). If God the Father wanted to simply bring condemnation on the earth, he could have done it long-distance without the involvement of Jesus. Instead, our loving heavenly Father sent Jesus to love and save, redeem and restore. God does not operate from a spirit of condemnation. That is not his basic nature. No doubt God is holy, righteous, and pure. Yet our heavenly Father has an enormous capacity to forgive his wayward children and receive them back into his fellowship.

This is not to say that God never judges. When people suppress the truth about God, exchange it for a lie, and bring condemnation on themselves by refusing to be adopted into his family through Christ, they *will* face condemnation. But that is not Paul's audience here. He is talking to believers who have stumbled, who have fallen into discouragement; to believers who have been victimized by the evil one, who is busy intensifying their shame, guilt, and remorse so that they become incapacitated, useless, and stuck in a perpetual penalty box. To these people Paul is speaking the truth that they are not to live under condemnation.

(cont.)

Our failures, shortcomings, sinful thoughts and deeds don't have the power to separate us from God's love. We are inseparable, and the Father who sent Jesus has open arms and is always ready to welcome us home. It does not matter how far we have wandered or how much we have sinned. The Father is ready to forgive, restore, and celebrate our homecoming. We must never underestimate the depth of the Father's love for his children. Once a Father ... always a Father. Once a child ... always a child.

Read Romans 8:1; John 3:16 – 17; Psalm 103:11 – 13; and Luke 15:11 – 24

7. In light of the teaching of these passages and others in the Bible, what is the basic disposition of God's heart toward those who have come to him by faith in his Son, Jesus Christ?

8. Imagine you could live each moment of your life with an abiding and profound conviction that God loves you with never-ending passion and looks at you with the eyes of a grace-filled Father. How might this reality impact *one* of the following areas of your life?

   • How you look at your own children

   • How you care for strangers in need

- How you deal with a person who has wronged and hurt you

- How you make time to be with God throughout the day

- How you worship when you are gathered with God's people

- How you share God's love with the people in your life

The Work of the Holy Spirit ... Getting Back in the Game

At the moment in time we trust Christ as Savior and Forgiver, we become a child of God. In that very breath the Holy Spirit—God's internal presence—moves in to begin his work of transformation, and we never have to live with God's condemnation again.

The same Spirit who brought Jesus back to life now gives us life, making us responsive to God, giving us power, giving us spiritual gifts, imparting love for people, granting us peace that passes human understanding, and so much more. As we recognize the presence and power of the Spirit that dwells in us as God's children, we won't want to spend another second in the penalty box. There is too much to do, and wasting time sitting on the spiritual sidelines of life is simply not an option.

Read Romans 8:5 – 11; 1 Thessalonians 1:4 – 10; Acts 1:8; and 1 Corinthians 6:19 – 20

9. What are some of the ways the Holy Spirit is working in the world, in your church, or in your life?

10. How does the Holy Spirit help us live free from condemnation and focused instead on the good works and ministry we can do?

Celebrating and Being Celebrated

The grace of Jesus sets us free. The love of the Father covers us. The power of the Holy Spirit fills us. We are no longer under condemnation. As a group, thank God for freedom from condemnation and the cleansing you have in Jesus. You might even want to start each prayer by personalizing Romans 8:1: "I am in Christ Jesus, therefore I live with no more condemnation. I celebrate that I have been set free from ..."

Loving and Being Loved

When we recognize the amazing grace we have received, our freedom from condemnation in Jesus, we want others to experience the same joy and confidence. If you have a friend or family member who has received Jesus, but still seems to spend a lot of time in the penalty box, share the freeing message of Romans 8 with them in the coming week and encourage them to get back in the game.

Serving and Being Served

Not only do we put ourselves in the penalty box through self-condemnation, but sometimes we do the same to people around us for the sins they commit. One of the best ways we can serve other believers is to make a decision not to put them on the sidelines because we heap condemnation on them. In the coming week, humbly ask God if there are people in your life that you have been putting in the penalty box. If he puts a person on your heart, commit to do four things:

1. Ask God to forgive you for bringing condemnation when he has declared "no condemnation."

2. Ask this person to forgive you. Share what you have learned in Romans 8 and admit that you realize you have been condemning them.

3. Commit to a "no condemnation" lifestyle that will protect you, and those around you, from ending up in the penalty box.

4. Evaluate your heart at least once a month. If you are shifting back into condemnation mode with those around you, go back to number one and start over.

Confident Christians

ROMANS 8:12–17

In some Christian traditions and circles, the idea of being confident is frowned on. Too much confidence is seen as pride. Followers of Christ with such bold assurance are considered a bit arrogant or suspect.

Yet, according to Romans 8, the God who declares that nothing can separate us from his love wants us to live with an unyielding confidence that we are his precious children. Writing to the Christians in Rome, the apostle Paul wants to clear up any remaining doubt and confusion that sometimes hangs over believers' heads like a dark cloud, and so he lays out some of the indicators, some of the marks, which accompany a true faith in Christ.

God wants the issue of Christian confidence to be settled so that we can get on with the task of living for him. A lack of confidence in our salvation, an uncertainty of the power of Jesus in our life, or a waning assurance of God's love ... these things are not signs of spirituality, they are a recipe for disaster.

God wants you to be confident in your salvation, tuned in to the presence of Jesus in your life, and absolutely assured that you belong to your heavenly Father. His love for you is so great, and his grasp on your life is so secure, that you and he are truly inseparable! You can live with an unbending confidence of this reality.

Making the Connection

1. Finish *one* of following statements:

    • When I was growing up, being boldly confident was considered ...

- One thing that has helped me grow confident as a follower of Jesus is . . .

- One thing that can erode my Christian confidence is . . .

- If I wanted to encourage a Christian whose confidence was waning, I would tell them . . .

Knowing and Being Known

Read Romans 8:12 – 17

2. Imagine you are in a season of life when you lack confidence as a follower of Jesus—perhaps you have lingering feelings that God doesn't love you, or you feel distant from him because of guilt and struggle. How might this passage speak comfort, hope, and confidence to your heart during a time like this?

The Work of the Spirit

The first indicator of our salvation that Paul lifts up is the presence and power of the Holy Spirit in our lives. As we see the Spirit at work, we can be confident in our Christian faith.

Not only does the Holy Spirit regenerate and make us responsive to God, but he undertakes our ongoing transformation. This includes identifying sinful attitudes and actions that might have gone unchecked or unnoticed for a long time. When the Spirit is at work in us, these behaviors come to the surface and we say to ourselves, "This stuff has to be dealt with. I need to change. Spirit of God, help me repent and become more like Jesus, even though it might be hard or painful." One confidence-building indicator that the Spirit is at work is a desire to change, grow, and turn from sin.

We also see the Spirit's presence when we notice the fruit promised in Galatians 5 growing in our life. This typically takes time, just as it takes time for a tree to produce an orange or a vine to grow grapes. But as we look at our hearts and lives and see increased patience, deeper love, more consistent self-control, more peace in the hard times, and so on, we can be confident we belong to Jesus. Along with this, we discover joy and meaning in using our Spirit-given gifts to minister in the church and the world. We don't feel pressured or coerced to serve, but it becomes a delight. And we notice an increasing desire and boldness to tell others about God's love and to serve them in ways that will show the presence of God in the world. All of these become positive indicators that the Holy Spirit is alive in our lives.

Read Romans 8:12 – 14; Galatians 5:19 – 26; and 1 Corinthians 12:4 – 11

3. Recall a time when you felt and followed a deep conviction of the Spirit to change or repent. Describe how this process assured you of God's love and commitment.

4. What is one fruit of the Spirit that is already growing in your life, and how does this realization increase your confidence that God is working in you?

    What is one fruit of the Spirit you would like to see cultivated in your life, and how can your group members pray as you seek to grow in this area of your spiritual life?

5. What is one gift of the Spirit that God has placed in you, and how are you using it for his glory? How does this ministry grow your confidence that God is alive in your life?

The Spirit of Adoption

A second indicator that should increase our confidence that we are inseparable from God is the awareness that we are loved and adopted children of our heavenly Father. The Greek language has two words for "father" that are used in the New Testament, one more formal and the other more intimate and personal. The intimate word, *Abba*, was the one our Savior used when he cried out to the Father in the garden of Gethsemane and said, "Abba, Father, everything is possible for you. Take

(cont.)

this cup from me. Yet not what I will, but what you will" (Mark 14:36). This word is more like the English "Daddy" or "Papa."

Not only did Jesus use this informal, intimate term, but the apostle Paul tells ordinary people that they can and should refer to God this way as well. What a shock, but what a blessing and source of strength. And one that we should not neglect in our own lives today.

Paul teaches that the Holy Spirit changes the nature of our relationship with God from one of fear and slavery to assurance that we are loved and adopted sons and daughters. The Spirit bears witness with our spirit that we are no longer slaves or hired hands, but children of our loving Abba. That's a confidence builder!

Read Romans 8:14 – 16; Galatians 3:26 – 29; 4:4 – 7; Hebrews 12:7 – 11; and Psalm 27:10

6. The message of Scripture assures us that God is a tender and loving Father, and that all Christians are loved and adopted daughters and sons. How do these passages push back on the notion some people have that God is an angry father, or that he is constantly disappointed with us?

7. Tell about a season of life when you lived with a deep, personal awareness of God's "Abba" fatherly love for you.

How did this understanding impact your confidence as a Christian?

8. What are some things we can say and do to help others grow in their awareness that God loves them as a consistent, tender, and caring Father?

Enduring Hardship for God's Glory

A third source of confidence that we are truly followers of Jesus is our attitude and disposition when we face times of suffering and hardship. The way a Christian responds to the reality that following Jesus involves sacrifice is radically different than the perception of those who are not yet his followers.

Most people outside the family of God think in terms of the minimum requirements needed for getting into heaven. They would like to live as they please, be comfortable, and still escape hell. Those who have not seen the face of Jesus and stood at the foot of his cross can't imagine why anyone would willingly suffer for him.

The true believer says, "I don't care what it costs, I'll follow wherever God leads. It doesn't matter how he wants to use me ... I'll face suffering, embarrassment, and offer my very life for the One who gave his life for me." When that kind of attitude is growing in our heart, it is an undeniable mark of genuine faith.

Read Romans 8:17; I Peter 2:19–21; 4:12–16; and Philippians 1:29–30

9. What do these passages have to say to people with the following attitudes?

    • Non-Christians who are considering the Christian faith but want assurance that following Jesus will guarantee the promise of a "good life," without suffering

    • Christians who are disappointed with God because they have been "faithful" but are still facing loss, pain, and suffering in life

10. Describe a time you endured hardship because of your commitment to Jesus and how this experience impacted your faith.

    How can these times serve to either strengthen or weaken our faith?

11. What suffering, struggle, or hardship are you facing today, and how can your group members support you and help you grow deeper in faith through this time?

Celebrating and Being Celebrated

Followers of Jesus can have absolute assurance of their salvation. They identify the worth, vitality, and newness of life which the Holy Spirit's presence brings; they see themselves as God's children and God as their Abba; and they are increasingly willing to endure hardship, if called upon by God.

Quietly reflect on the ways you see God at work in your life, then as a group offer prayers of celebration using one of the following prompts:

- Spirit of God, I celebrate your presence and power in my life. I can see you at work . . .
- Abba, Father, I rejoice in your tender love for me and celebrate the way you . . .
- Lord Jesus, you suffered for me and now I give you thanks that I have the honor of facing hardship in your name. Help me honor you as I face . . .

Loving and Being Loved

Take time this week to express your love and deep appreciation for your Abba Father. Write a Father's Day card to God, pouring out your heart with childlike honesty. Simply begin, "Dear Abba . . ."

Serving and Being Served

When the apostle Paul wrote about the reality that we share in the sufferings of Jesus, he did not express this sentiment as a theorist or theologian. He did so as one who had suffered staggering pain for the sake of following Jesus. This week read Paul's own account of what he experienced as he followed and served the Savior in 2 Corinthians 11:21–29.

After reflecting on Paul's life-story, in silent prayer pledge your heart and life in service to God, even when it is hard, even when it is inconvenient, even when it means suffering. Thank Jesus for suffering for you and commit to follow him, no matter what the cost.

Only One Life

ROMANS 8:18–27

Only one life will soon be past, only what's done for Christ will last." I was just an adolescent when I heard those words for the first time. They caught me up short, as I was struck with a profound awareness that not everything I do will last into eternity. "Could it possibly be," I asked myself, "that without careful and prayerful consideration, I could live an entire lifetime on this earth and end up empty-handed in eternity, with nothing to show for my activities and pursuits when I finally see God face-to-face?" I just kept thinking, *What a tragedy that would be.*

All those years ago I was fairly self-aware. Though not on the fast track to becoming a Rhodes scholar, even I knew that I would be spending a whole lot more time in the next life than I would ever spend in this one. So I began thinking about which life I should concentrate and focus on. I could pursue and seek after the things that were crying for my attention in this life ... and there were plenty of them. Or, I could make a conscious decision to invest my heart, mind, soul, and strength in things that will make an eternal impact.

Decades have passed since I first heard those haunting words, "Only one life will soon be past, only what's done for Christ will last." As I look back, I can honestly say that I have tried to invest my one and only life in the things God says will last forever. In retrospect, I wouldn't have it any other way!

Making the Connection

1. What are some of the pursuits in this life that can cry for our attention and dominate our schedule but have very little impact on eternity?

What can we invest ourselves in during this lifetime that will yield eternal dividends?

Knowing and Being Known

Read Romans 8:18–27

2. Paul starts this section of Romans 8 by declaring that the sufferings of this life can't even be compared to the glory that awaits us. How can this spiritual truth help a follower of Jesus evaluate how they are investing their life?

How can the suffering in this life actually help a person focus more on the eternal and less on what this world offers?

It Will All Be Worth It ... You Can Bank on It!

Paul paints the picture with bold, broad strokes. No matter what we face in this life, no matter how bad it seems, no matter how much it hurts, no matter how deep it cuts, the glory of heaven will one day make these sufferings seem small. He is not saying that our struggles do not matter or that our losses are insignificant. He is not declaring that God does not care about our pain and suffering. What he *is* doing is drawing a contrast. Compared to all that awaits those who follow Jesus ... compared to the glory that is just on the horizon, compared to these things, there is no comparison!

For those who set their hearts on the eternal glory of God, for those who run the race set before them, for those who strive to gain the eternal prize, there is great news! Paul says, "It will be worth it all. When we contrast the hardships of this life with the glory that awaits us, heaven wins every time. Trust God. You can bank on his goodness and promises."

In many ways, every follower of Jesus is building their whole life on this promise. We are counting on the fact that someday the record books will be opened and the ledger sheets that tell the real story are going to be totaled. On that day God is going to say, "Well done, son. Well done, daughter. You ran the right race. You now receive the imperishable wreath. You didn't choose to go the instant-gratification route. You didn't lead a life of self-indulgence. You lived with one eye on eternity and you made tough choices. It has all been worth it and great is your reward."

Read Romans 8:18 and 1 Corinthians 9:24 – 27

3. Paul paints a picture of two races in which we can compete. One involves a crown that does not last and the other a prize of eternal value. In light of this imagery, discuss the following as it relates to the race God *wants* his people to run:

   • What does this race include?

• What is the right way to run this race?

• What are the prizes for competing in this race?

4. Paul talks about strict training and beating his body into shape so he can run the race victoriously. What are some of the *practices* or *disciplines* we can incorporate into our lives that will serve as training tools so that we can stay in spiritual shape and run this race to the end?

Name one spiritual discipline or practice you need to develop in your life. How can your group members pray for you and cheer you on as you seek to develop this training tool?

Hang In There ... Stay Faithful!

Speaking as a spiritual father and friend, Paul cheers on those who follow Jesus. He knows the journey gets hard. He understands the temptation to give up. He too has felt the burden of carrying a heavy load for Jesus and knows how the weight can feel crushing. So he urges them—and us—to hang in there, to stay faithful ... even when things get difficult.

If you listen closely, you can almost hear Paul's words of exhortation ringing through the centuries: "Listen to someone who knows what he is talking about. Listen to someone who has traveled the road, suffered deeply, and has come out on the other side more in love with God and confident that it will all be worth it. Whatever price you are paying to follow Christ, whatever it costs you to stay true to him, however much heat and heartache you absorbed in order to follow the Savior, stay faithful! God will see to it that you will be compensated in eternity in multiplied form. You are running the right race. Your heavenly portfolio is growing daily. Your heavenly Father is smiling. Hang in there!"

When the cross of Christ gets heavy, when the rigors of righteous living get exhausting, when the responsibilities for discipling people get overwhelming, when the weight of serving others gets discouraging, when the sacrifices of giving money get tiring, when attempts to lead people to Christ seem futile, endure and press on. The light and momentary affliction that you are experiencing at this moment is producing for you an eternal reward that is beyond your wildest dreams. Stay in the battle. Remain faithful!

Read Romans 8:18 and Hebrews 12:1 – 3

5. The writer of Hebrews gives wise advice to help followers of Jesus remain faithful in the spiritual journey. Share how *one* of these ideas has helped you hang in during a difficult time:

   • *Remembering we are surrounded by a great cloud of witnesses* —Picturing that those who have gone before us (friends, family members, and the great men and women of faith throughout history) are watching and cheering us on

- *Throwing off the sins and things that weigh us down* — The process of confessing, repenting, and getting rid of baggage that keeps us from running the race as we should

- *Fixing our eyes on Jesus* — Remembering what he suffered and endured for us, and letting that be a model and source of inspiration as we run the race

6. Tell about a time when you felt tired, discouraged, and ready to drop out of the race, but you pressed on and felt God's presence and power carry you forward. What kept you running?

What counsel would you give to a Christian who is feeling discouraged, ready to drop out of the race and spend time on the sidelines?

7. What are some of the situations you face that can lead to discouragement, slow your pace, or force you out of the race God has called you to run?

8. If you are facing a time like that right now, share your challenge and how your group members might encourage and pray for you as you seek to remain faithful to God's will in your life.

Help Along the Way

We have one life to live for God ... only this one life. When we make the decision to pursue the things that last forever, that have eternal impact, we are on the right track. When we purpose in our heart to run the race, eyes fixed on Jesus, and remain faithful to the end, heaven notices! At these pivotal moments we realize that the inseparable love and presence of God is ready to help us move forward. At every moment the Holy Spirit is filling us, empowering us, and interceding for us in perfect harmony with the Father's will.

When we feel weak and even our prayers are faint, we don't have to worry. In these times we can remember that God knows us in all of our humanity and he says, "Some of you beat yourselves up because your prayers aren't strong enough. I don't want that to separate us. My Spirit, who knows your heart better than you do, will pray on your behalf." Just think about it. God even helps us pray when we don't know what to say. What comfort! What strength!

Read Romans 8:26 – 27

9. According to this passage, what is the Holy Spirit's unique ministry when it comes to our prayer life, and how does this truth bring hope and encouragement?

10. We all face times when we don't know how to pray. In these moments we are not alone. The Holy Spirit comes near and prays for and with us. One way God can minister to us in these times is through the Spirit-led prayers of his people. If you have hit a roadblock in your prayer life, share this with your group and allow them to briefly pray for you right now.

Celebrating and Being Celebrated

In Romans 8:18 – 27, the apostle Paul acknowledges that followers of Jesus will face suffering and struggles, but he also brings good news for those who know the Savior. As a group, express prayers of praise and celebration for these good things:
- The glory that awaits us is greater than any suffering this world can bring
- The Holy Spirit intercedes for us and expresses what we cannot
- Through Christ we are experiencing, and will one day fully realize, what it means to be adopted as God's children

Loving and Being Loved

God longs for all of his children to make a radical shift in their values and priorities. He wants us to stop running in a cheap race, looking for cheap thrills, and competing for a cheap prize. Instead he wants to see us enter the real race, the eternal race, and compete for the real prize ... an imperishable wreath. He wants to see us start focusing on building heavenly portfolios and less on having it all here and now. He desires his beloved children to grow more in love with him. Since the first and greatest commandment is to "Love the Lord your God with all your heart and with all your soul and with all your mind" (Matthew 22:37), one of the best things we can do is pour our energies into this pursuit.

Find a quiet place and time in the coming week and talk with God about your relationship with him. Ask him to help you:

- Worship with greater passion,
- Live for him with deeper devotion,
- Converse with him more often,
- Be mindful of him and his will throughout the day,
- Yield yourself to him with every ounce of intensity you can muster, and
- Use your gifts and abilities for his purposes in greater measure.

Serving and Being Served

I once heard a speaker say, "All Christians should identify anything we get too attached to and put a red tag on it with the word 'temporary.' This will remind us that none of the stuff of this world is going to last forever; we are not going to take it with us."

As an act of devotion to God and service to others, take a walk around your home and mentally put red tags on everything. As you survey furniture, clothes, vehicles, and the very structure in which you live, mark it all "temporary." If you come to something that makes you pause and say, "I don't want to put a tag on this," do it anyway! Then commit to serve others by sharing and using your temporary stuff in a way that honors God and blesses others.

Our Lifeline in Times of Trouble

ROMANS 8:28

It is an old, familiar story, one we have all heard and lived. It is a season of life when you are feeling close to God — trusting him, living clean, sensing his blessing. Then the phone rings and a voice says, "Are you sitting down?" Or a registered letter arrives and something in your gut knots up before you open it. Out of the blue the HR director calls you into her office. The police knock on your door at 3:00 a.m. and you do a lightning-quick mental inventory of which family member is not home.

In the space of time it takes a human heart to beat, everything in your life can be turned upside down. In that moment you think, "This cannot be true. Not me. Not us. Not now. God, where are you?"

In the middle of loss, pain, adversity, senseless violence, and the brokenness of this life, God's Word speaks: "And we know that in all things God works for the good of those who love him, who have been called according to his purpose." Sometimes Romans 8:28 is an immediate source of hope and comfort. At other times it can stretch our capacity to believe. We can find ourselves wondering, "How can this turn into something that's good? Really? How can God possibly bring good out of this? I just don't see it!"

Making the Connection

1. Tell about a time you faced sudden pain, loss, or suffering, but were carried forward with a firm confidence that God would bring something good out of a bad situation.

Or, tell about a time when pain, loss, or suffering came crashing in unannounced, and you found yourself feeling, "God, there is no way anything good could ever come out of this."

Three Places We Live: BP, IP, or AP

All of God's best people have experienced suffering and struggle; the Bible and history affirm this truth again and again. The question is not, "Will I ever experience pain?" but, "How will I respond when pain comes into my life?" All of us live in one of three primary locations in relationship to pain.

The first is BP or **Before Pain**. Some people actually get to live the first ten or twenty years of their life without experiencing any kind of debilitating tragedy or loss. For those who are still in this season, Romans 8:28 might feel a bit theoretical, but it's a truth they must accept nevertheless.

The second location is IP or **In Pain**. People in the midst of adversity must hear Romans 8:28 and muse, "If that verse weren't in my Bible, I would think the world is completely out of control. Even with that verse, there are moments I wonder if it is possible that God can bring something good out of what I am facing today. But I'm going to hang on and do all I can to trust God despite this pain." Romans 8:28 can become a lifeline in these times.

Finally, many people are living AP or **After Pain**. They have walked through the fire and come out the other side with a glimpse of God's glory. It is not that everything makes sense. But they have a deepening awareness that God has taken something from the dunghill of pain and evil and grown a beautiful thing that can bring him honor and even bless other people. For those who are living on the other side of pain, Romans 8:28 is a treasure.

The sobering reality is that this life takes us through a cycle of living BP, IP, and AP. At any given moment, a faithful follower of Jesus can be in any of these three places.

Knowing and Being Known

Read Romans 8:28

2. What does this passage reveal about:

- God

- Our circumstances

- Us as followers of Jesus

What Romans 8:28 Is *Not* Saying ... All Things Work Out

Romans 8:28 has been so twisted and misused over the years that it is important to clarify exactly what it is *not* saying. This verse does not say that all things are guaranteed to work out; it can't be sculpted into a promise that every story will end with a "happily ever after." We do not live on such a planet, and God's Word never ensures that all circumstances will work for our pleasure or comfort, or add to our net worth.

Instead, this verse says that the transcendent God, the Creator of the world, the all-powerful One who raised Jesus from the dead, gets elbow-deep in the storyline of your life. He supernaturally weaves the events, even the tragedies, in such a way that at some point you will look in the rearview mirror and be able to say, "As awful and as painful as that era was, I can now see that God brought some good out of it."

Read Romans 8:28 and I Peter 1:6 – 9; 3:14 – 17; 4:12 – 16

3. What does Peter teach us about the reality and place of suffering in the life of a Christian?

4. What might the apostle Paul or Peter say to *one* of the following people?

    • A new believer who declares, "I'm so glad I'm a Christian because now God will protect me from all suffering and pain"

    • A nonbeliever who says, "If there really were a loving and all-powerful God, he would remove all suffering from the face of the earth"

    • A Christian who asks, "Why would God allow me to go through this time of pain and suffering?"

What Romans 8:28 Is *Not* Saying ... God Causes All Things

Romans 8:28 is *not* saying that God causes all things. Although God is sovereign and all-powerful, other forces are still at work in the universe. Sometimes we face suffering and pain because of the presence and work of Satan. Sometimes we are hurt by the choices of other people. Sometimes we suffer because of natural disasters that come with living in this physical world. To top it off, we can make poor choices and cause our own pain. God does not want the blame for these things and we should not give it to him. Doing so becomes the source of much disappointment and disillusionment.

Read Romans 8:28; Genesis 3:1 – 7; and John 8:44; 10:10

5. How does the presence of Satan and his work in this world account for much of our pain, suffering, and evil? What examples of suffering appear to originate from the hand of the devil?

6. Much of the suffering we try to blame on God is the result of unwise and sinful choices made by people. Strangely, even those who claim they do not believe in God (and prove it every day by the way they live) are quick to blame him when things go wrong. List examples of how we can face suffering and pain in this life because of the sinful and unwise actions and decisions of:

    • Family and friends

    • Governments and groups of powerful people

    • Our own choices and decisions

7. How does our outlook on suffering change when we admit that much of what we face comes from Satan, other people, our own choices, and natural disaster?

What Romans 8:28 Is *Not* Saying ...
All Things Bring Good for Everyone

Romans 8:28 does *not* say that God works for the good of everybody who walks the face of the earth. Though God is loving and longs that all people would come to faith in him, this verse does not guarantee the same work of God for all people. There is a special way that God brings good out of evil and broken situations for those who are called his children.

When you begin a relationship with the heavenly Father through faith in Jesus Christ, he extends you a special provision. You have entered a new life and are called according to his purpose. No matter what you face, God can bring good out of it for his glory! Those who are still on the other side of the cross do not have this same assurance.

Read Romans 8:28

8. Those who have come home to their heavenly Father through faith in Jesus Christ can live with confidence that God can bring redemptive grace into the worst situations. Those who are not followers of Christ do not have this hope. How might this reality become a fresh new motivation to reach out with the good news of salvation found in Jesus Christ?

Think of one person in your life who could really use the hope found in Romans 8:28. How can your group support you in your efforts to communicate God's love and message of hope to this person?

What Romans 8:28 *Is* Saying

Romans 8:28 is a mind-blowing promise that no matter what pain, suffering, or loss you face in this life, God will eventually weave it into something that brings glory to his name and goodness to this broken world. You might look back and still call a tragedy a tragedy. The memory of what you felt or lost could still bring tears to your eyes and somberness to your heart. But though you may never fully grasp the *how*, you will realize that our gracious and mighty God has brought good out of evil, hope out of pain, glory out of loss.

9. Describe the good God has accomplished through a tragic and painful situation in your life.

10. If you are right in the middle of an IP (In Pain) time of life and can't see the other side of the suffering, share this with your group members and allow them to pray for God's presence, strength, and hope to fill you.

Celebrating and Being Celebrated

We all travel the landscape of suffering in our lives, whether we are currently Before Pain, In Pain, or After Pain. As a group, use the three seasons of suffering to direct your prayers of celebration:

Before Pain (BP)

- Thank God for a season when pain, loss, and struggle is not in the forefront of your mind.
- Celebrate that whatever comes your way, your faith in Jesus can never be taken away. What matters most is made secure through your relationship with the Savior.

In Pain (IP)

- Rejoice that Jesus is with you no matter what you face or experience in this world.
- Thank God that he never lets you go or abandons you, even when you might feel far from him. Celebrate the rock-solid truth that nothing can separate you from God's love (Romans 8:39), that no one can take you from the Father's secure hand (John 10:28–29).

After Pain (AP)

- Thank God for carrying you through the fire and helping you make it to the other side.
- Celebrate that God can bring good out of even the worst of life-situations.

Loving and Being Loved

Both the Old and New Testaments clearly teach that suffering is part of the journey of following God. The idea that "good Christians" will never suffer is a contortion of Scripture and diametrically opposed to life experience.

In the coming week, read Isaiah 43:1–3 three or four times, slowly and reflectively. Notice each time the passage says, "When . . . ." Observe where God is during the times of deep waters, raging rivers, and burning fires.

Pray that you will learn to recognize God's presence in life's hard times, that you will be able to hear his voice and feel his touch even when the storm is raging. As the years pass and you become more assured that God is with you in difficult days and can bring good from them, pray that you will be able to express confident love to him even then.

Serving and Being Served

In light of the lessons you learned in this session, consider doing one or more of the following suggested activities:

- *Share* with others the message of salvation in Jesus and the hope we receive through a relationship with him. Identify people you know who have faced hard times and let them know there is a God who can bring good out of the worst this life can bring.
- *Pray* for those who are going through times of loss, pain, and suffering. Ask God to reveal himself to them, even in the midst of pain, to give them glimpses of how he can bring good out of what seems like a hopeless situation.
- *Tell* stories of how God has brought good out of the hard life-experiences you have encountered. In particular, share these stories with children and teenagers who might still be on the BP side of this equation. Let them know that you have seen God carry you through dark and painful times and even bring good from situations you were sure could only bring pain and sorrow. Your testimony will help prepare them and provide hope for their future.

God Is for You

ROMANS 8:31–34

God is for you. He really is! The apostle Paul declares it with Spirit-anointed boldness: "If God is for us, who can be against us?" No matter where you are in your journey of faith, God is cheering you on and longing for you to take the next step.

The Journey

Christ-Centered Christian
▲
Growing Christian
▲
Beginning Believer
▲

✝

▲
Explorer

Explorer. Someone who's investigating Christianity is trying to figure out if the puzzle pieces fit together in a way that would make this faith system believable, one they can embrace. When these people read Romans 8:31 and hear that God really cares about Christians, it is still just theory. In their mind it might be true, but they have not personally experienced this heavenly love and goodness.

Beginning Believer. When a person receives the grace offered in Jesus Christ and enters God's family by faith, they become a beginning believer. Their sins are forgiven, the Holy Spirit blows into their heart like a fresh wind, and everything becomes new. As they take baby steps of faith, they start to experience this wonderful truth that God is for them. Day by day they discover the reality of God's care and love, his support and strength.

Growing Christian. As the months and years pass, this beginning believer matures into a growing Christian, profoundly aware that God is for them and ready to help them in every area of life, whether the issue is resisting temptation, building healthy relationships, or walking in obedience to biblical teaching.

Christ-Centered Christian. The shift from a growing Christian to a Christ-centered Christian comes when a person freely surrenders their desires and dreams to the will of God. At this point, they experience a whole new level of trust and growth; their primary concern becomes God's program and his purposes for their life. Christ-centered Christians declare with resounding confidence, "If God is for me, who can be against me?"

Making the Connection

1. Describe some of the characteristics that mark the life of a person who is:

   • An explorer

   • A beginning believer

   • A growing Christian

   • A Christ-centered Christian

2. What are some of the things that will help a person take the next step forward in the spiritual journey from:

- An explorer to a beginning believer

- A beginning believer to a growing Christian

- A growing Christian to a Christ-centered Christian

- A Christ-centered Christian to a more mature and committed Christ-centered Christian

What are some of the things that might cause a person to stall on their spiritual journey?

Knowing and Being Known

Read Romans 8:31 – 34
3. What are some of the things God has done, is doing, and promises to do in the future that bring assurance that he is truly for us?

God Is for You ... More Than You Know!

There's no one else on planet Earth that God wants to help more than you. There's nothing in God that would make him want to withhold something that would be good for you. Because of the price Christ paid for your redemption, God's inclination is to listen to you, care for you, and help you. He is for you!

Sadly, too many followers of Jesus think that God is out to get them. They see him as an angry judge who can't wait to slam down his gavel and scream, "Guilty." This is *not* the picture your heavenly Father wants to rule your mind or guide your heart. God is always accessible, available, and open-armed. He wants you to know that he will be at your side, no matter what you face.

Read Romans 8:31 – 34 and Luke 18:1 – 8

4. If we compare God to the hard-hearted judge of Luke 18, what logical conclusions might we draw about him?

On the other hand, if we see the judge in the parable as a contrast to God (exactly the opposite), what lessons about God might we learn?

5. Many people wrongly interpret this parable as a comparison, but it is meant to show contrast. What are some of the negative and false pictures of God that people carry in their heart?

Why is it so important to purge our hearts and minds of the false pictures of God painted by culture, the media, and even poor biblical interpretation, and live with the understanding that God is for us?

God Is for You ... In Every Situation

God is not just for you in some ethereal, spiritual way that makes you feel all tingly inside but does not impact your daily life. This idea of God being "for me" is central to *practical* biblical theology. When we embrace this truth, it changes everything about how we approach life. An assurance of God's support, love, and presence impacts our attitudes, motives, and actions.

6. How might a person's confidence that God is for them impact *one* of the following life situations?

    • When a parent is dealing with a child who is rebelling and resisting things of faith
    • When a person is in a difficult marriage and they feel ready to give up on the relationship
    • When an employee feels unappreciated, undercompensated, and begins thinking about ways they might cut corners to "even things up"

- When a person has been hurt and is having a hard time extending forgiveness
- When someone is facing an ongoing temptation that feels like it will never go away

7. Name one area of your life in which you are not feeling God's presence, strength, and support. How might things change if you had a deep, profound sense that God is for you and with you in this situation?

When We Get It Wrong

God is for us, no doubt about it. But if we are not careful, our tendency toward sin and self-centeredness can twist this beautiful truth and turn it into a trap. We can end up believing that God promises to give us whatever we want and to do whatever we tell him. We can think that God is for our all-American dream, guaranteeing us the big promotion, the fancy award, the financial windfall. Rather than being the Lord of our life and the universe, we reduce God to a divine errand runner for our personal agenda.

8. What potential dangers or pitfalls ought we to expect if we begin to interpret God being "for us" in the way described in the box on page 59?

How have you seen people (including yourself) fall into the trap of believing it is God's job to give us whatever we want?

Sold Out and Surrendered

Christ-Centered Christian
▲
Growing Christian
▲
Beginning Believer
▲

✝

▲
Explorer

Some people think the biggest chasm between these phases of the spiritual journey is the one that separates "explorer" and "beginner believer." To be sure, this is a large chasm that only Christ can bridge. But, as the years pass, I am discovering that a huge chasm also exists between a "growing Christian" and a "Christ-centered Christian." To make this jump we must be sold out and radically surrendered to the Holy Spirit, and that's a leap many believers fail to take.

God's vision to redeem and restore a broken world goes far beyond the vision of self-interest and personal promotion that many of us, Christians included, content ourselves with. This vision will only become a reality when followers of Christ enter a level of spiritual devotion that includes self-surrender, complete obedience, and a willingness to suffer—a commitment to take up the cross of Jesus every day. Christians who only ever get to the point of trusting God to help them with their own program, needs, and desires miss out on the adventure and glory that a life of mission, service, and sacrifice demands.

Read Philippians 1:20 – 26; Acts 20:22 – 24; and Luke 9:23 – 25

9. What can help propel a follower of Jesus into a life of radical trust, sacrifice, and service?

What gets in the way of us living with this level of devotion?

10. Tell about a person you know who has lived a Christ-centered life of devotion that has included willing sacrifice and humble service.

What did you learn about the Christian faith from this person, and how has their example of faith inspired you?

11. What is standing in the way of you taking the next step forward in your Christian journey? How might the members of your group cheer you on and pray for you as you seek to surrender more fully to Jesus?

Celebrating and Being Celebrated

As a small group, lift up prayers of praise and celebration for God's commitment to his children ... including you. Use some of the following prompts to guide your prayer time:
- Thank God for how he leads people forward through the various stages of faith and growth, from explorer to Christ-centered Christian.
- Praise God for the people he has placed in your life who have been an example of maturity and a source of inspiration as they have modeled what it means to be a Christ-centered Christian.
- Celebrate how God helps you in every life-situation and how his presence guides and strengthens you.

Loving and Being Loved

We all have a handful of people God has placed in close proximity to us who have been an example of a radically surrendered Christ-centered Christian. Take a moment to write down their names here:

Commit to affirm and bless at least one of these people this week by sending a note, email, or text message, or by making a phone call. Let them know how their life has inspired you as a model of true surrender to Jesus. Thank them for letting the Holy Spirit work in them in such a way that they have become an example to you and others.

Serving and Being Served

A Christ-centered Christian is committed to doing God's will and serving humbly, even when it is hard. In the coming week, reflect on your walk with Jesus and identify (in the space below) one or two areas where God might have prompted you to serve or sacrifice, but you opted for a less rigorous pathway.

Now, pray for a fresh passion and commit to act on the Spirit's prompting. You might want to share this commitment with one of your small group members who can pray for you and keep you accountable to follow through.

More Than Conquerors

ROMANS 8:35–39

What does it mean to be a conqueror? And what does a person who is, in the words of Romans 8:37, "more than a conqueror," look like? Does it mean marching around thumping our chest? Is it about making triumphant predictions that we're going to take over governments, nations, and eventually the world? Does it mean we can do whatever we want without fear of repercussion or consequence? Is it about being in control, on top, always self-assured? No, these things do not mark the life of a person who is more than a conqueror.

A man or woman who lives as a conqueror in Jesus Christ understands that they can experience daily victory and obedience that was never a possibility before the power of God was unleashed in their life. Conquerors say no to the endless little temptations that pop up every day, even when no one will ever see or know what they did. They love their kids and pray for them in the middle of the night when bodies are weary and minds are numb. They hang in there and humbly serve a spouse who is dealing with sorrow, depression, and deep pain. God's conquerors do business with honesty even when it costs them a deal or a client. They study hard for a big test even when someone offers to give them the answers and guarantees an "A." Conquerors make space and time to sit at the feet of Jesus, feed on the Word, and talk with their Lord even when schedules are busy and other things cry for their attention.

Every time a follower of Jesus makes a decision to be a Christ-centered Christian and follow God's will, heaven looks on with pride. These men and women are truly conquerors, indeed more than conquerors.

Making the Connection

1. Tell about a sin, struggle, temptation, or attitude that you could never seem to overcome until you became a follower of Jesus.

How did God's power in your life and your relationship with Jesus help you overcome in this behavior?

Knowing and Being Known

Read Romans 8:35 – 39
(Have the leader or a volunteer read the passage, slowly and clearly.)

2. In this passage, the apostle Paul names one after another of the strategies and tactics the enemy uses to defeat us and make us feel distant from God. Give a personal example from the following list:

- Troubles and hardships
- Persecution
- Economic struggles
- Wars and conflicts with people

- Facing death (yours or that of someone you love)
- Demonic attack
- Fear of the future
- Other ways Satan tries to make us feel defeated

3. Using the same list from question two, how have you seen God's power unleashed in your life as you have experienced being an overcomer in one of these areas?

Attitude Check: Overcomer or Victim?

We live at a time when playing the victim is quite common, blaming others is a standard tactic, and complaining is chronic. This mentality can even creep into the lives of Christ followers, especially beginning believers —whether at home, the workplace, or at church. This is *not* God's plan for his children.

Christ-centered Christians face the same struggles, but their attitude is radically different. Instead of complaining, grumbling, and declaring themselves the "victim," these overcomers press on, live with hope, and cling to the promise that nothing could ever separate them from God's love. How can they do it? Because they believe the teaching of Scripture, not just in theory, but also in the nitty-gritty realities of daily life.

Read Romans 8:35 – 39

(Provide a couple of minutes of silence for group members to read the passage through silently.)

4. In light of this passage, what might the apostle Paul say to a Christian who has a pattern of complaining about all the "tough breaks" they face or whining about how hard their life is?

More Than Conquerors in Our Spiritual Lives

The Bible teaches that something very powerful ought to happen when we have a growing and dynamic spiritual life: we begin to live as a conqueror. This happens as we commit to regular learning times with God's people, whether at worship services, in small groups, or through other such opportunities. It also includes growth in personal spiritual disciplines, such as Bible reading, prayer, journaling, silence, and fasting.

The enemy will do everything in his power to disconnect us from Christian fellowship and personal spiritual disciplines. But in the overcoming power of Jesus, we are more than conquerors. We can choose to make space for God, growing closer, going deeper, discovering the joy of our salvation.

Read Romans 8:35 – 39

(Have a volunteer read verses 35 – 36, pause for a few moments of silence, and then continue reading verses 37 – 39 in response to the question posed in the first section of the passage.)

5. What are some of the ways the enemy tries to push us away from community with other believers and commitment to

personal spiritual disciplines? How can we resist these tactics and remain a conqueror in the development of our spiritual lives?

6. What spiritual practice or discipline has been waning in your life, and what steps can you take to get back on a Christ-centered track?

More Than Conquerors in Our Vocational Lives

A more-than-conqueror kind of person, an overcoming Christian, deals with work challenges and realities without complaining or playing the victim. If they get a new boss who is kind of tough, they don't grumble to other employees. Instead, they fall on their knees and pray, "God, show me how I can build a relationship with my new boss. Fill me with your love so I can love my new boss. This person is someone made in your image. I'm not going to fall in line with everyone who's complaining. I just won't do it." If they find out that their skills need to be sharpened — and they would normally fume about the extra load — instead they say, "God made me to be a growing person. If I need to read a book, take a night class, or update my skills in some way, in the power of Christ, I will overcome my complacency and add value to this organization. And I'll do it with a good attitude!" This is the response of a Christ-centered employee who understands what it means to be a more-than-conqueror kind of person in the workplace.

Read Romans 8:35 – 39

(Read this passage on your own and personalize it: "Who shall separate me from the love of Christ … No, in all these things I am more than a conqueror …")

7. Our vocation is what we do each day, for most of the day. In this setting, we can live as a joy-filled person who is confident in God's overcoming power, or we can settle into an apathetic and mundane routine of doing the least work possible. What does an overcoming and Christ-centered person look like in *your* place of vocation?

How are you seeking to avoid the pitfalls of the defeated victim mentality and grow as a conqueror in your vocational life?

More Than Conquerors in Our Family Lives

Some of us live with bitterness against family members that we have turned over and over, like meat on a rotisserie grill. We claim to be a growing Christian, we want to be a Christ-centered Christian, but we just can't seem to forgive and move on. Feeling stuck and defeated, we're certainly not conquerors.

It's time for us to move beyond victim to victor in our family life. God didn't save us and forgive us so that we would end up in the jail of unforgiveness; he saved us so that we would be an overcomer, fully surrendered to him and free from the petty stuff that tears families apart. Even pain that has built up for years can be healed and new beginnings can come. This is the hope we live with when we are more than conquerors.

Read Romans 8:35 – 37

(Have one person volunteer to read just verses 35–37.)

8. What are some of the common places of family dysfunction and brokenness that can drag a Christian down to defeat?

9. How have you experienced the overcoming power of God unleashed in your family, and how does this give you hope for future healing and victory?

More Than Conquerors in Our Daily Lives

Every day we shop in stores, go to meetings, get on airplanes, interact with neighbors, and interact with other people in numerous ways. Every one of these daily-life experiences can be an opportunity to show that we are God's conquerors!

- When someone cuts in and grabs a parking space we were waiting for (and our signal was blinking … indicating that we were planning on taking that spot)
- When our flight is delayed and we have to stand in line to get a new ticket
- When a server in a restaurant seems cranky and inattentive
- When we can't find the TV remote

- When a person in the grocery store has twenty-three items in their cart and they are in the ten-items-or-less aisle right in front of us
- Whenever the weather is bad and the sky is cloudy
- When someone in the fast lane is driving the actual speed limit
- When the baby goes to the bathroom a few seconds after she's been changed and redressed
- Whenever a person who grates on us walks into the room

These moments, and countless others like them, are opportunities to prove that we are more than conquerors. It is in the furnace of daily life that we are refined, tested, and can come out like pure gold!

Read Romans 8:38–39

(Have the group leader or a volunteer read just verses 38–39.)

10. What are some of life's little irritations that can set you off and challenge your overcoming spirit?

The next time you face this challenge, what can you do to show that you are truly an overcomer in Jesus Christ?

Celebrating and Being Celebrated

As a group, lift up prayers of celebration for the overcoming power of God in your lives. Also praise him for his love that makes you and him inseparable, no matter what this world throws at you!

Loving and Being Loved

God showed his love to us by forgiving our sins, and now he calls us to follow his example. If you have a family member who has wronged you in some way and you have not yet forgiven them, consider heaven's act of love and extend grace, whether or not you feel they deserve it. You might want to read and reflect on the following passages before you proceed: Matthew 6:9–15; Colossians 2:13–15; and Ephesians 4:32. Ephesians 4:32 would be great to commit to memory if you feel called to become more of a conqueror in the area of forgiveness.

Serving and Being Served

Identify one of your pet peeves, something that really bugs you. (If necesssary, use some of the ideas expressed in question ten to get your juices going.) Then write down what it is that bothers you here:

Next, write down ways you could serve the very kind of person who drives you crazy:

For instance, if you get irritated with people who drive too slow in the fast lane—and your normal MO is to speed up behind them, flash your lights, and then race around them—maybe you could serve them by committing to pray for them as you pass (and skipping the impolite driving behaviors besides!).

Session One – The No Condemnation Concept
ROMANS 8:1–11

Question 1

This can be a very vulnerable question. The idea is not to be specific about sins, but to acknowledge that we tend to condemn ourselves and place ourselves in the penalty box. The idea of the penalty box will carry through this whole session, so be sure to read it in advance to understand how the concept is developed and how it relates to Romans 8:1.

Questions 2–3

This passage in Romans makes it crystal clear that God does not condemn those who are in Christ Jesus. And if God does not condemn us, who are we to condemn ourselves? Christ has dealt with our sin on the cross. It is gone.

Here in Romans, as well as elsewhere in the Epistles, the apostle Paul draws a vivid contrast between a life lived according to our sinful nature and a life guided by the Holy Spirit of God. Take time as a group to dig into these contrasting lifestyles.

For another passage that draws out a similar juxtaposition of life in the flesh (sinful nature) versus life in the Spirit, you might want to read Galatians 5:16–26.

Questions 4–6

The evil one loves to make a bad situation worse. Guilt, remorse, and shame are the normal results of wrongdoing, but according to Revelation 12:10, we know that Satan continues to accuse us. This means that one of his strategies is to take the normal guilt or remorse that comes from wrongdoing and to intensify it, exaggerate it, push it to the limits.

The evil one knows full well that a thoroughly discouraged Christian is an utterly useless Christian. So, whenever a believer does something he or she regrets, the evil one swings into action immediately and starts intensifying the shame. God says, "No condemnation," but the enemy has other ideas. The accuser lies and says, "Now you've done it. That was the last straw. God is fed up with you. His patience has ended. His grace is used up. He is sick and tired of your stupid mistakes, weary of your premeditated foul-ups and sins. No amount of pleading or penance will ever be enough to make God change his mind about you. You are history, out of the family. Give it up. You are condemned. See you in hell."

I have bought those lies ... hook, line, and sinker. You probably have too. I once met with a leader who counsels people with compulsive behavioral patterns and addictions. I asked him, "How much guilt do those courageous brothers and sisters, who are trying to work through some of those problems, deal with on a daily basis?" The guy rolled his eyes and he said, "Try truckloads. They live with it all the time. They get up in the morning feeling condemned and they go to bed at night feeling even worse. They are Christians hanging by a thread—defeated, demoralized, sure that God has no use or love for them."

They are wrong! God does love them, Jesus died for them, and the Spirit is ready to lead and use them. When we are in the penalty box and feel like this, it is time to turn to Romans 8 and get back to the basics!

Questions 7–8

God's love is bigger than we can imagine or dream. The Father is looking down the road, expectantly waiting for any prodigal son or daughter to come home. When we do, he runs—not walks—to us and embraces us with grace. As we read Romans 8 and other Bible passages, we see a picture of a Father who sent his only son as the sacrifice to wash away our sins and restore our relationship to him. When we understand this, we realize that he also loves those around us, which in turn ought to impact the way we treat and forgive them.

Questions 9–10

Some people say you can be a Christian and not have the Holy Spirit. They explain that it might take a month or a year or five years, but then you get the Holy Spirit through the laying on of hands, and have evidence of his presence by speaking in tongues. This is simply not biblical. When you trust Christ as your Savior, the Holy Spirit immediately takes up residence within you. If the Holy Spirit isn't evident and active in your life, the flat truth is you are not a Christian. If there is no transformation happening, if there are no promptings, no assurances or guidance, no work or witness of the Holy Spirit, this text says it is because you are outside the family of God and you need to be saved. If you will let the Holy Spirit be free in his ministry in your life, the same remarkable kind of life that Jesus Christ led will flow in and through you. This is good news.

Session Two – Confident Christians
ROMANS 8:12–17

Question 1

God is not looking for arrogant and prideful children, but he *does* call us to have humble confidence in him. That's the point: our confidence and assurance are not in our gifts, abilities, or strength, but in his sufficiency and power.

When we see his Spirit alive and moving in power, we grow in confidence. As we learn that our heavenly Abba loves us with unending passion, assurance increases. In the challenging times when we endure hardship in the name of the Savior, we know we are his people. These things help us grow into confident Christians.

Question 2

It would be nice to travel the road of life and faith and never deal with doubt. It would be amazing to never experience wavering confidence. But all of us have moments when the enemy whispers in our ear, "You blew it! God can't forgive that. You have crossed the line." In these moments we can hold tightly to these words in Romans. God's Word gives assurance and hope to us when our knees tremble and insecurity sets in. No matter how we might feel, the Spirit is with us, we are still children of a loving Father, and he will carry us through whatever we might face. We can be confident that nothing can separate us from the love of God that is found in Jesus Christ.

Questions 3–5

Can you identify the regenerating work of the Holy Spirit in your life? Or, do you feel cold and unresponsive to the Spirit's work? If you can sense the Spirit's presence and are different now than you were before you trusted Christ, Paul says this spiritual reality ought to give you a strong measure of assurance that you are indeed a member of God's family.

Not only does the Holy Spirit regenerate us, but also he transforms us. Note that Paul writes about the Spirit putting to death the deeds of the body and how this reveals that we are children of God. As we look back a week, month, or year and see the changes the Spirit of God has made in our lives, our hearts should soar in confidence.

True Christians can identify the work of the Holy Spirit. They have the sense that they are being regenerated, revitalized, being made more responsive to God. A kind of reconstruction or remodeling is ongoing and they celebrate it.

When the Holy Spirit is at work within us, he strips away the old stuff—sinful thoughts and behaviors—and encourages us to walk in newness of life and purity. He calls us to reconcile broken relationships and encourages us toward tenderness in all our relationships. Our old desires are passing away, replaced with his desires.

Questions 6–8

People outside the family of God might respect him and hold him in high esteem, might display a kind of reverence toward him, might even go to his house now and then, but only true believers relate to him as Father and feel the freedom to call him "Dad."

Some time ago our son, Todd, was on an ocean crossing, traveling the South Pacific on a small sailboat. He had just finished another thousand-mile passage and, to be quite honest, I was thinking about him often, praying for him and wondering how he was doing. When our phone rang at home that Friday night, in my heart I lifted up a brief prayer, "O God, please ... this could be good or bad. Please let it be good news about Todd." Sure enough, it was him! "Hi Dad, I'm doing great!" I let out a quiet sigh of relief. There was something powerful about hearing my son's voice.

Every time we say to God, "Hey Dad, it's me ... just checking in," it blesses the Father's heart. When we stop to lift up a prayer such as, "Abba, I'm just thinking about you. I wanted to say hello. I'd like to tell you about my day. I'd love to have a brief conversation with you," he is delighted to hear our voice. Just as I felt with Todd, God cares for us more than we can imagine.

In this passage Paul emphasizes one of his all-time favorite "before and after" comparisons. He reminds readers (then and now) that they used to picture God, in their pre-Christian days, as a distant, demanding, and detached employer (or slave owner). But when they came to faith in Jesus Christ, an absolutely remarkable change happened. They could now see God as an affectionate, approving, and accepting Father who gives permission to call him Dad. True believers feel the Father's concern and compassion, devotion and provision. True believers feel like beloved sons and daughters.

Questions 9–11

We of all people should view the term "halfhearted Christian" as an oxymoron. It should not compute in our brains. How does a person who claims to be a Christian yawn at nail-pierced hands and feet? How does a person who claims to be a follower of Jesus look at a blood-stained cross and say, "Who me, serve? Who me, tithe? Who me, risk a little ridicule from a fellow worker by witnessing on the job? Who me, visit a prison, work in a food pantry, assist the poor or elderly?"

Paul says that it is normal for a Christian to be willing to endure hardship. It is one way we can say, "Thanks, Lord, for your amazing grace. I regret that I only have one single life to give back to you for all you have done for me." The apostle Peter was severely beaten for telling others about his faith in Jesus Christ, yet before his wounds had time to heal, Scripture tells us (Acts 5:41) that he rejoiced because he was considered worthy enough to take a beating for Christ. Paul was beaten and imprisoned, yet could sings songs of praise, rejoicing that he could share in Christ's suffering. It is this Paul who reminds us that part of following the Savior is being willing to share in his suffering.

If there should be any group on planet Earth that burns with zeal, that shares it message with tenacity, and that meditates on the goodness of God day and night, shouldn't it be Christians? Shouldn't it be us? Shouldn't we look at our Savior's hands and feet, gaze into our heavenly Father's eyes, ponder what is awaiting us in eternity, and realize that anything we might suffer in this life will pale in comparison to the glory that awaits us?

Session Three – Only One Life
ROMANS 8:18–27

Question 1

Most of what we seek after and pursue is not going to last forever. Many of these things are not bad, they just aren't eternal. If we want to get our hearts, minds, and schedules oriented around that which is eternal, we need to remember the words of Jesus when he was asked what is the greatest of all the commandments. He replied:

"'Love the Lord your God with all your heart and with all your soul and with all your mind.' This is the first and greatest commandment. And the second is like it: 'Love your neighbor as yourself.' All the Law and the Prophets hang on these two commandments." (Matthew 22:37–40)

Jesus emphasized that God and people are what will last forever. This is where we should place our energies, how we should invest our lives. When we do, we are on the right track.

Question 2

Paul is making a simple but profound statement. If we could take the weight of all our suffering and struggles of this life and place it on one side of some giant scale, then place the glory that is awaiting us as children of God when we get to heaven, the scales would always tip toward the glory we will receive. The weight of glory is so much greater that there is really no comparison.

Of course, there will be moments (hours, days, weeks) when this will not feel the case because we have not yet tasted the full goodness and glory of God. But the truth remains even when it is hard to comprehend. When our hearts embrace this spiritual reality, we get a whole new perspective on suffering. We also find ourselves committing to invest our one and only life in the things that matter most to God and less on the transitory things of this world.

Questions 3–4

In 1 Corinthians 9:24–27 we learn that there are two races every human being has the opportunity to enter. The first race is an earthly one and the passage likens it to training for the Olympics.

In this race we train, practice, and spend a lifetime preparing to compete for a perishable wreath, a prize that will wilt in a matter of hours or days. This is a picture of how we can fill our hours and days seeking things that might be fun, nice, even harmless, but they do not last forever.

There is another kind of race we can choose to enter. It is a heavenly pursuit. When we train, practice, commit ourselves to winning this race, God offers an imperishable wreath, a reward that goes into eternity and lasts forever. This is the race God invites us to sign up for.

There are many ways to train for this second race: studying God's Word, going deep in prayer, learning to fast, seeking God through solitude, committing to service, worshiping wholeheartedly are among the spiritual disciplines and practices that will pave the way to victory. Paul lets us know that a regimen of strict training and submission of our lives to God's will is part of the package. This is a core element when it comes to being a follower of Jesus.

Questions 5–8

A great cloud of witnesses is surrounding each of us — cheering, rejoicing, praying, spurring us on. We might not be able to see them or hear their cheers, but they are real! Sometimes it helps to imagine this crowd ... to think about those who have gone before us, those who ran hard and crossed the line, who understand what we are going through. Perhaps we'll picture a faithful Christian grandparent or the apostle Paul himself urging us on from the grandstands of heaven. As we hear them cheer, "Hang in there, it will all be worth it," our hearts should be stirred.

We are also called to travel light. In the times when we feel it is hard to run the race God has set before us, we should examine ourselves to see if we are trying to run with a hundred-pound backpack of disobedience strapped on. Confession, repentance, and casting sin aside are what we need to do in these moments.

Maybe the most inspiring thing we can do as we seek to run the race of faith is to look hard at the finish line and see Jesus standing there with his nail-pierced hands stretched out toward us. As we fix our eyes on him and remember the race he ran for us, the price he paid, we can press on and live the life he has given us to the fullest!

Questions 9–10

What a comfort and hope we have in the Holy Spirit. Even when we run out of words and do not know how to pray, the Spirit steps in and prays for us. What a reminder that we are inseparable from God. He even prays when we come to the end of ourselves. What an inspiration to keep living this one life we have for the glory of God.

Session Four – Our Lifeline in Times of Trouble
ROMANS 8:28

Question 1

This session expands on one key verse of the Bible: Romans 8:28. The focus will be on not only what the verse says, but on what it *doesn't* say. For example, it doesn't say that God works all things for our comfort or our pleasure or our net worth, or even that he works for the good of everybody. It *does* say that God can bring change or good even out of pain that is being experienced by those who love him. God wants his children to know they are inseparable from his loving heart, and this passage is a great reminder of this truth. Even in the times of our greatest pain, sorrow, loss, and suffering, God is looking for ways to bring good into our lives. That is an inseparable love.

Question 2

God is at work. He is active, on the move. No matter what we might face, his inseparable love drives him to bring something good out of the hardships of this life. Even if we end up in a painful situation because of our own rebellion or sin, God can still bring good out of it. Even when the enemy of our soul attacks and seeks to hurt us, God is so committed to his children that he can bring good from these situations. The God who calls us to follow him is deeply committed to our good.

There is nothing we face that God does not see. He is aware of our struggles and pain. This does not mean he will always remove them. It does mean he will be with us no matter what we face.

As followers of Jesus, we can know for a fact that we are loved by God, our heavenly Father. And so we can live with confidence in the promise that he can bring something redemptive, good, and honoring out of the worst of situations.

Questions 3–4

Some people try to comfort themselves and others by saying, "It will all work out!" or, "Things always work out for the best."

This is not true, and it is certainly not the message of Romans 8:28. The Bible does not promise that everything will somehow magically work out in a way that pleases us and makes us happy. As a matter of fact, sometimes things might end up exactly the opposite of what we think would be best and good. Sometimes things end up bad, sad, and painful. Yet God is saying to his people in this passage that he can accomplish amazing and good things through very bad situations.

Questions 5–7

The Bible *does not* teach that God causes everything that happens in the universe or in our lives. The Bible *does* teach that God is sovereign, powerful, and loving. But other forces are at work, and God does not always intervene and stop bad things from happening. What are some of these forces that can bring about pain, suffering, and loss in the world?

Satan: The Scriptures are very clear that an evil force is at work in this world. He is called, among other names, Satan, Lucifer, the devil, the evil one, and the tempter. John 10:10 says the evil one comes to kill and steal and destroy. His strategic plan is to throw wrenches into our lives that will lead to heartache of every kind imaginable.

Natural Law: Living in a fallen cosmos also causes suffering and pain. Rising tides, airborne diseases, the laws of physics and gravity and economics, and so much more create great grief and struggle in this life. When people build homes along the edge of a river that typically floods every six years, is it really an act of God when their living rooms end up under water?

Other People: Because we live in marriages, in families, in communities, the choices of others can hurt us. When a man or woman says, "Until death do us part," and then walks away from a marriage because they no longer feel satisfied, that choice hurts a spouse, kids, family, and friends. When someone gets drunk and drives a car, they endanger themselves and others. This is not the doing of God.

Personal Sins: Let's be honest and face up to the fact that much of the suffering we face in this life is self-induced. When we make unwise choices, act on sinful impulses, and rebel against God's will, it always ends up in pain. This is our own doing, not the work of God.

Question 8

God holds a special place in his heart for those who are his children. This is not to say that God loves only certain people. It was God who so loved the whole world (John 3:16) that he sent his only Son to die for our sins. God loves all people and Christ died for all who will receive and believe.

But when a woman or man opens their heart to receive Jesus by faith, a new kind of relationship is forged. We become children of the almighty God, a part of his family. He watches over us in a special way. When this happens, God guarantees that no matter what we might face, he can bring good out of it. It does not matter if the suffering was self-induced, caused by Satan, or the result of a natural disaster. In all things God can work good ... for his called and chosen children!

Questions 9–10

Some years ago I was traveling in the Far East and got a virus that made me sick for nine months. I went to the Mayo Clinic twice and found myself thinking, "I don't see how anything good can come out of this." Because many of the medical reports were very troubling, I began to wonder if I might not be nearing the end of my journey on earth. But God in his grace restored my health, and I can now look back and honestly say that much good came out of my time of deep struggle.

For one, God gave me a *new sensitivity* to other people's health issues. Church staff used to call me to say they weren't coming to work because they weren't feeling well. I'd think, "Suck it up. Get in here. We all get a sniffle now and then." But during my illness, I couldn't always suck it up. Since then, when I hear of someone who's struggling I think, "It must be so frustrating to want to go places and do things and not have the energy to do it. I understand now." God used my illness to give me greater compassion and make me a better pastor, father, and husband.

Another good thing God did through my illness was that he *unified our family*. My kids were praying for me. They would call and say, "Praying for you, Dad." Lynne would do the same.

When I realized that I needed my wife and kids to minister to me, I began to understand family and community in new ways. God used a bad situation that lasted a long time to grow this reality in my heart. These are just a couple of examples from my own experience, but I share them to encourage you that God can bring good out of your hard times as well.

Session Five – God Is for You
ROMANS 8:31–34

Questions 1–2

Along the continuum of spiritual growth, perhaps the hardest step to take is from a growing Christian to Christ-centered Christian. This session encourages us to take hold of the promise of Romans 8:31 and integrate that spiritual reality into every situation of daily life. Being willing to give up our self-centered programs and getting on God's program will likely mean a little inner turmoil, but getting on God's plan will fill the void of anything that we have to give up, and he will always be there in support along the way.

On this journey there will be people, situations, and truths that propel us forward. There will also be obstacles, pitfalls, and things that cause us to stall. The key is that we keep pressing forward so that we become Christ-centered Christians who keep growing in maturity. At the start of this session it might be helpful to read Philippians 3:12–14 and see the example of the apostle Paul:

Not that I have already obtained all this, or have already been made perfect, but I press on to take hold of that for which Christ Jesus took hold of me. Brothers, I do not consider myself yet to have taken hold of it. But one thing I do: Forgetting what is behind and straining toward what is ahead, I press on toward the goal to win the prize for which God has called me heavenward in Christ Jesus.

Question 3

In this brief passage we are reminded of the price God has paid to prove that he is for us—his one and only Son, Jesus. God's love for us is so great that he did not spare what was most precious to him. We are justified in Jesus and free from all charges and accusation that might come from people or even the pit of hell. In Christ we are cleansed.

Along with the infinitely valuable gift of salvation in Jesus we discover that God will graciously give us all things. This is a picture of the generosity of God, who is eager to provide for his children. It is not a promise that every hedonistic whim we have will be satisfied.

In addition we are told that Jesus, even now, is at the right hand of God interceding for us. What assurance and hope this should bring us when we face the harsh struggles and realities of this life.

As your group ponders these wonderful truths, you could also briefly expand your discussion to the teaching of the whole Bible and consider all that God has done, is doing, and promises to do in the future for those he loves.

Questions 4–5

One of the most colorful parables that Jesus ever told is found in Luke 18:1–8. Jesus describes a judge quite graphically: he doesn't honor God and he doesn't respect people. In other words, this man has a lot of power but no moral imperative. A recipe for disaster.

The other main character in this parable is a widow. In the day Jesus told this parable, widows were typically poor, disconnected, and powerless. This particular widow has a problem: she's being oppressed. The only one who can help her is the judge. Another problem.

Despite the widow's frequent visits to plead her case before this judge, he basically tells her each time to get lost. So she puts together a strategic plan that goes something like this: "I'm going to become this judge's worst nightmare. I'm going to show up every day, so often that I'll wear him down and force him to help me." And, sure enough, the judge finally gives in out of sheer exhaustion and frustration with her.

If we didn't read further, we could easily conclude that Jesus is saying that we are like the widow and God is like the judge. As a matter of fact, many have interpreted the parable this way: God is this being who really doesn't want to bother with penniless and powerless people like us; we are an irritation to him. The only way to get him to help us is to pester, harass, and bug him until he is so sick of us that he gives in to our demands. What a sad picture this would be!

But if we *do* read further, we discover that Jesus actually flips the message and informs the reader that this story is meant to illustrate that *God is totally unlike the judge*—and we do not have to be like the widow. This parable is a contrast, not a comparison. The message is that God's basic inclination is to bless and help his children. We are not powerless, penniless, and disconnected; we are not strangers before some heavenly court. We are loved and adopted sons and daughters. We can call God Abba ... Father. God is for us!

Questions 6–7

There are all sorts of examples of how knowing God is for us can shape and impact the way we live. Here are just a few brief ones:

When you're going into a tough meeting at work and you're hoping the presentation goes well, you can remember, "God is for me in this process. He wants me to do my best, and he's going to help me." Then, you can lift up a childlike prayer to Abba, who has promised you his calming presence.

You need to have a tough talk with your teenager. You think, "The stakes are so high. I hope I don't mess this up." In that moment you can remember, "God is for me in this situation, cheering me on. He cares about my teenager more than I do. I can do this ... in his strength and with his help."

A powerful temptation confronts you. You think, "I hope I can fight this one off. If I fall, I will feel horrible in the morning. I don't want to dishonor God and give in." God is for you in that moment. Listen and hear him saying, "I don't want you to fall. I'm for you. My Son died and rose again to unleash the power you need to say no. My Spirit lives in you. Let's handle this one together. I'll give you the strength."

If we can integrate this spiritual reality into every situation of life, we will be amazed at the power God gives. In every situation we can declare, "God is for me in this, cheering me on. I don't have to figure out how to get his attention and whether or not he's with me. I already know and can press forward with confidence."

Question 8

In much of Western culture, the biblical truth that God is for us has been twisted. The enemy has taken this beautiful assurance and turned it into a recipe for self-centered living. Instead of living with the assurance that whatever we face, God is with us, ready to help us through, we can begin to use this truth as a license to believe that God must give us whatever we want. And so we can behave like spoiled children in a candy shop yelling, "Give me, give me, give me!" This is not the point at all. Sometimes the most loving answer a parent gives a child is no.

Questions 9 – 11

The apostle Paul declared that his life was not about his personal program, desires, and whims (Philippians 1:21). Nor was it about getting more money, greater pleasure, or more of life's "good stuff." Instead, he understood that following Jesus just might mean surrendering his whole life, even to the point of dying for his Savior. What a refreshing perspective in a time when some preachers tell people that God's primary job is to bless them and meet their every desire.

I think back to when I became a Christian late in my teenage years. I learned about Christ's work on the cross and how his sacrifice resolved my sin problem, if I would only believe and receive him. I learned that through humility and repentance God would accept me into his family and invite me to call him Father. He would help me, give me strength beyond my own, guide my life, and secure my eternity. What an amazing gift I received from the hand of a loving God.

Where did this gift cost me? What was I giving up, other than a little pride that I thought I could save myself? It did not cost me much to come to faith in Jesus and surrender to him. But it cost Christ a lot. He left the glory of heaven, was rejected, abused, beaten, and crucified. He took my sins on himself and paid the ultimate price—death on the cross.

How can I *not* follow him? How can I *not* surrender my plans for the sake of following his? With all he has done for me, it is a small thing for me to commit to live as a Christ-centered Christian and offer all I have and am to the One who gave everything for me.

Session Six – More Than Conquerors
ROMANS 8:35–39

Question 1

Romans 8:37 says, "In all these things we are more than conquerors through him who loved us." Our God, who never wants us to be separated from him, offers us the power of Christ that we might have the ability to overcome things we couldn't overcome without his strength. In this session we learn that committing to God's program and immersing ourselves in the spiritual disciplines prepare us to carry that conquering spirit into every circumstance of life. As we do, we will discover what it means to be fully Christ-centered.

In Christ, we are inseparable from God. This is a fantastic concept. The God who made the universe wants to have an intimate bond with us. He says, "I know you're going to mess up. I'll forgive you. Let's walk together. I know you're going to get scared. I'll help you face your fears as you keep your hand in mine. Let's walk together. I know you're not going to pray as much or as wisely as you should. I'll cover you. I'll send the Holy Spirit, who will help give expression to what you can't express. Let's walk together." What a God we serve.

Questions 2–3

You will note that only one passage is used in this session and you are being asked to read it over and over again. This is intentional. This is such a rich and nuanced passage that reading it several times will reveal its various facets. The "reader" suggestions are offered as ways to keep the reading fresh. Feel free to use these or come up with your own.

As you prepare for this session you might want to read 2 Kings 6:8–23 (particularly verses 15–17). This is the powerful Old Testament story about Elisha and his servant.

Question 4

Beginning believers or growing Christians can buy into the victim mentality and become grumblers and complainers—it's not a pretty sight! God wants to move us past these childish ways and grow us up into maturity.

Christ-centered Christians have learned a bit about suffering, struggle, giving up their program, and following God no matter what. These believers seek to walk in victory and keep a Christ-honoring attitude no matter what they face at home, work, church, or elsewhere. Christ-centered Christians become a witness to the power of God wherever they go. They stand out because the attitude and Spirit of Christ is strong in their life.

Questions 5–7

The Bible knows nothing about a Christ-follower who functions in the markeplace like every other person without faith. The Bible just assumes that the work of the Holy Spirit—through your small group, your spiritual practices, and your church worship—is going to catalyze something significant within you and impact who you are on the job.

If someone on your work team is telling dirty jokes, instead of running to your church and applying for a job to get out of that filthy world you have to be a part of Monday through Friday, an overcomer says, "God, there's a reason why this person tells these kinds of jokes. It's indicative of a heart far from you. Maybe the reason you moved this person to my team is because you want to use me to build bridges of friendship. Maybe I'll be the one who leads that person to faith." You can play the victim at work, you can call a foul on God, and you can whine and moan. Or you can take the Romans 8:37 approach and know you're more than a conqueror when God is with you.

Questions 8–9

Often home is the one safe haven where we can really be ourselves. Among other family members we can let down and show our true colors. But sadly, for this reason, our family members just might be the people who get the worst of us.

It does not have to be this way. Being more than conquerors should apply everywhere, including at home. If we are in the habit of revealing a very different side of who we are to our family members, one we would never show in public, it just might be time for God's overcoming and conquering power to transform our home life.

Question 10

Many of life's biggest tests come in the ordinary tasks of daily life. The moments that define greatness and uncover our true character come on as we drive down the road, stand in line to buy a gallon of milk, care for our kids, face unexpected delays, deal with difficult people, and do the stuff of normal life. As we become conquerors in these places, the big stuff will follow.

We value your thoughts about what you've just read. Please share them with us. You'll find contact information in the back of this book.

WILLOW
Willow Creek Resources

Willow Creek Association
Vision, Training, Resources for Prevailing Churches

This resource was created to serve you and to help you build a local church that prevails. It is just one of many ministry tools published by the Willow Creek Association.

The Willow Creek Association (WCA) was created in 1992 to serve a rapidly growing number of churches from across the denominational spectrum that are committed to helping unchurched people become fully devoted followers of Christ. Membership in the WCA now numbers over 12,000 Member Churches worldwide from more than ninety denominations.

The Willow Creek Association links like-minded Christian leaders with each other and with strategic vision, training and resources in order to help them build prevailing churches designed to reach their redemptive potential.

For specific information about WCA conferences, resources, membership and other ministry services contact:

Willow Creek Association
P.O. Box 3188
Barrington, IL 60011-3188
Phone: 847.570.9812
Fax: 847.765.5046
www.willowcreek.com

Share Your Thoughts

With the Author: Your comments will be forwarded to
the author when you send them to *zauthor@zondervan.com*.

With Zondervan: Submit your review of this book
by writing to *zreview@zondervan.com*.

Free Online Resources at
www.zondervan.com

Zondervan AuthorTracker: Be notified whenever your favorite
authors publish new books, go on tour, or post an update
about what's happening in their lives at www.zondervan.com/
authortracker.

Daily Bible Verses and Devotions: Enrich your life with daily
Bible verses or devotions that help you start every morning
focused on God. Visit www.zondervan.com/newsletters.

Free Email Publications: Sign up for newsletters on Christian
living, academic resources, church ministry, fiction, children's
resources, and more. Visit www.zondervan.com/newsletters.

Zondervan Bible Search: Find and compare Bible passages in
a variety of translations at www.zondervanbiblesearch.com.

Other Benefits: Register yourself to receive online benefits
like coupons and special offers, or to participate in research.